TRAVELING
STORIES
JOURNAL

A Guide to Discovering Your Own Life Lessons

TERRI CLEMENTS DEAN

TRAVELING STORIES JOURNAL:
A GUIDE TO DISCOVERING YOUR OWN LIFE LESSONS

LifeStory Publishing
P. O. Box 541527
Orlando, FL 32854

ISBN-10: 1939472202
ISBN-13: 978-1-939472-20-5

Printed in the United States of America

All featured quotes in this journal were written by the author and taken from *Traveling Stories: Lessons from the Journey of Life*.
Interior photos taken by author, her husband Mark, and a random stranger

Cover and interior design by Julie Valin,
  The Word Boutique, *www.TheWordBoutique.net*

First Edition: February 2015

10 9 8 7 6 5 4 3 2

For those who have stories to tell

NOTE TO READERS

There are really only four questions: Who Am I? Where Do I Belong? What Matters? How Do I live my life? Consciously or unconsciously, we spend our entire lives trying to answer them.

Consciously or unconsciously, we spend our entire lives trying to answer them.

We seek answers in many places. Sometimes our search takes us into foreign territories with strange customs or directly into the path of danger. Sometimes we are stuck at home with old answers that no longer satisfy. We may go to great lengths to learn our necessary lessons, but life itself is much more generous than we ever knew. She offers our lessons freely and without restraint, and these lessons make their ways to us in the small things, in the unexpected, in the struggles, and in the ordinary. Our task is to be impeccably honest with ourselves and pay careful attention. . . .

Our mission is to gather, to sort, to analyze, to engage, to allow ourselves to be taught. This is an act of individual choice and of personal will. Absolutely no one can do this for you, you are indeed on your own. It's often hard, and we weep with the sadness of our losses and tremble at the fear of the unknown. We long for easy solutions. We are shamed by our failures.

And we journey on. As we go, the pieces of truth collect around us, shape us, and orient us to the world. We are one, and we are part. We travel in knowledge and in mystery. It is the way of things, and it is good.

–Terri Clements Dean
Traveling Stories

CONTENTS

PART III: WHERE DO I BELONG?

PART IV: WHAT MATTERS?

PART V: HOW DO I LIVE MY LIFE?

EPILOGUE: TRAVEL WELL

*Life is both the gift and the teacher. That's where the lessons are and that's where
we make our offering in return. We simply must show up for life
and give it our best, day in and day out, year after year.*

INTRODUCTION

The pages that follow contain exercises meant to point the way to a deeper appreciation of the stories, which have helped shape you. It is my hope that working through this journal will enlarge and enliven your relationship with yourself and with your life. The exercises are drawn from stories in my book, Traveling Stories: Lessons from the Journey of Life, and each section includes quotes from the related chapter.

I have also given you many blank pages. Follow the path through this journal by completing the exercises, or feel free to bypass the exercises and simply tell your story on these pages. This journal is for you to use in the way that best fits your needs—write your story, draw it, make a collage of it, use fingerpaints or oils, words or images. The method is entirely up to you.

You own the story, and the story is important.

PROLOGUE

LIFE IS A JOURNEY

A TRAVEL STORY

But the journey is also the teacher, life's lessons freely offered and waiting to be learned.

Describe something unusual that happened on one of your trips.

Have you ever learned a lesson while traveling? Describe the situation and the lesson you took away.

What is a story about yourself that you love to tell?

So love your stories, tell them to the right people, and listen carefully when new stories come your way.

Notes

Additional Thoughts . . .

Life is a journey. The destination is both known and unknown.

PART I

THE JOURNEY

THE QUESTIONS

Pay careful attention to your stories.

How we travel matters to ourselves and to others. We must share our lessons and stories so others can hear and benefit from what we have learned. Within every individual story is the one story, the human story, the story that says I am human, I suffer, I endure, I hope, I dream, I fail, I carry on, I love, and I hope for love. We are the same with all our differences.

Make a timeline of your life so far. Add markers for ages as you wish; I do ten-year segments, but you might use five or two or twenty years. Then go back in your memory and note when big changes happened. You decide what counts as a big change. Be as creative as you wish with this exercise. Another possibility is to go through your life and note the predominant feeling/tone of each period—sad, fearful, hopeful, happy, etc.

Make a second timeline. Go back and ask yourself which of the four questions dominated:

Who am I?

Where do I belong?

What matters?

How do I live my life?

We can make the commitment to be steadfast in our quest for the answers that are right and true and honest.

Notes

THE LESSONS

If we listen carefully, we will hear life speaking to us. Our lessons are waiting.

Write one lesson you received during each of the time periods you selected on the timeline in the last section. How did it come? What happened? What did you learn?

There are many ways of learning—from books, from practice, from experience, from instruction, from modeling. How do you learn best? Give examples. Write about any struggles you have had with learning. What might have helped you?

Who were your best teachers so far? Write a memory about one or more of them and what you learned.

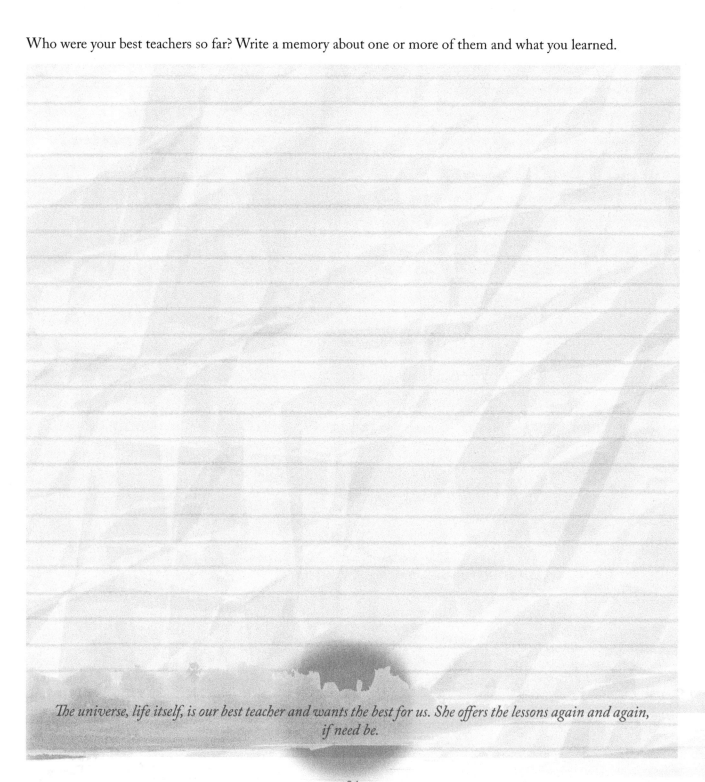

The universe, life itself, is our best teacher and wants the best for us. She offers the lessons again and again, if need be.

Notes

THE WORK

Life is both the gift and the teacher.

"The prerequisite for all growth and change is honesty." How do you relate to this statement? Has it been true for you? Has there been a time when being more honest with yourself opened the door for positive change in your life?

What does the phrase *trust the process* mean to you? Have there been times in your life when it was hard to trust? Describe a time when *hard work* has been required of you in order to move forward in your life.

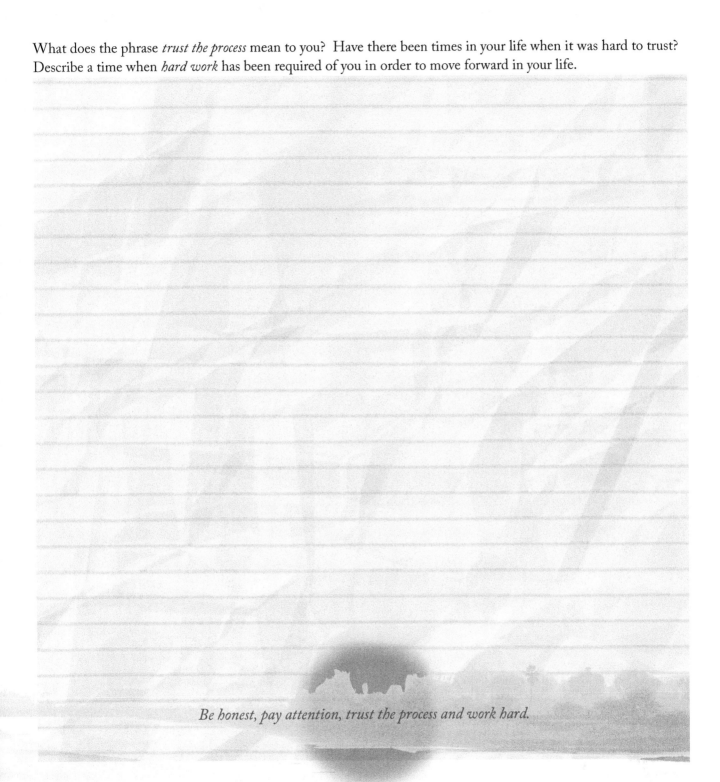

Be honest, pay attention, trust the process and work hard.

Notes

Additional Thoughts . . .

Life offers us every lesson we need for our journey, abundantly and without restraint. It's up to us to learn the lessons. In the end and all along, we are required to play our part.

WHO AM I?

ON STORY

The cure for what ails you begins with telling your story.

Write a short bio about yourself today, one that you might use on your website or on the cover of your book. What would you like people to know about you?

Now, write the most important things that you left out of that bio, but would tell your best friend or your therapist.

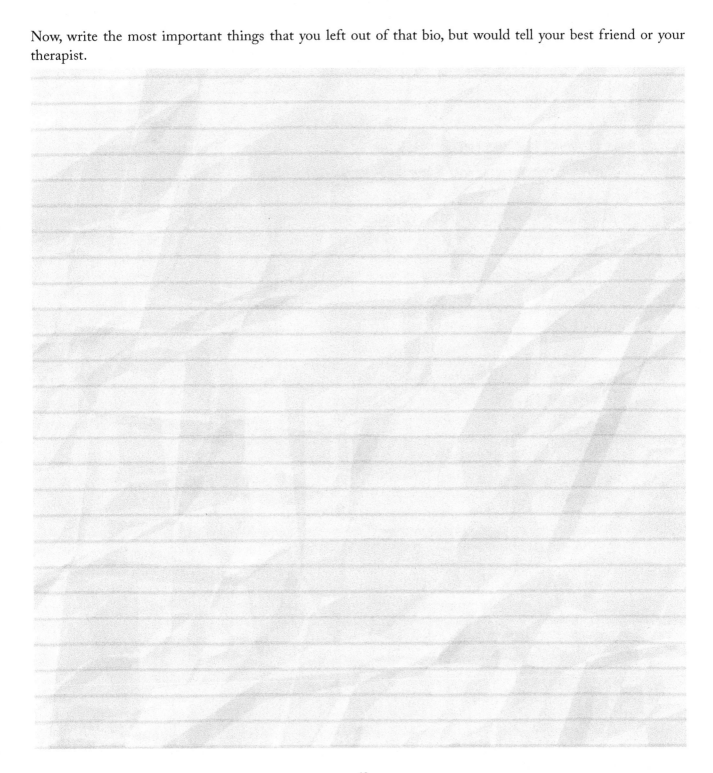

How old were you when you first:

Drove a car

Kissed a boy/girl

Noticed that someone was prettier/smarter/stronger/more talented than you

Took care of a child or a pet

Spent a night alone

Traveled alone

Said goodbye to someone important to you

Opened a checking account

Cleaned your own living space

Got in trouble

Wondered about God

Bought a car on your own

Signed a contract

Write a short story about one of those experiences. Pretend you are sharing that story with a friend. What would you tell him or her? Why is this event important to you?

Pay careful attention to your stories. They have power. They teach you what the world is like and what your part is in it. They can inspire you to create a better you and a better life.

Notes

WHO AM I?

We are each a living, breathing story in process with the authority to choose the next chapter.

Tell the story of your birth—who, what, when, where.

What is your earliest memory, the kind you can see in your mind's eye? Describe it in detail. Draw it or paint it. Try to make a one sentence statement about that memory or give it a title. How do you think that moment shaped your life?

This is a good place to add a photo or a drawing that represents that memory or from that time period.

Who am I?
Fill in the blanks in each statement. Don't edit, don't think, just respond.

I am

I am

I am

I am

I am

I am

I am

I am

Now go back and write a story about the person you described.

If you were to write your memoir or paint a painting that represents your life so far, what would the title be? What is the single most important thing you would want your audience to know about you? If it were to be a movie, who would you want to play the part of you? Why?

As an adult, have you learned anything new about yourself or a family member that surprised you? How did that feel? What happened next?

Who she is lives in the story; who she can and must become is already there as well, and all the healing she will ever need is also in the story, even though it is ongoing and ever-changing.

Notes

SLOWLY WALKING

Life is more fun when I act like myself and accept whatever situation that comes along for what it is.

Can you recall an experience when you learned to be more fully yourself? What did you learn? How has that changed your life?

Name five things you would surely do if they weren't so crazy, silly, outrageous, immature, socially unacceptable in your network of friends. etc.

1.

2.

3.

4.

5.

Assuming they fit with your morality, won't harm someone else, and aren't illegal or dangerous, try the least risky one. Write about what happens when you do that.

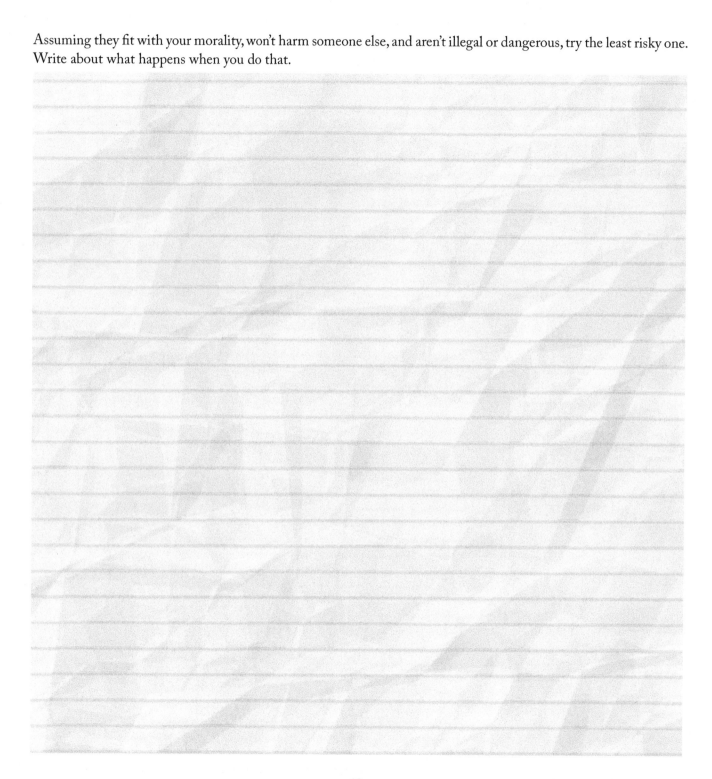

List five things that might be fun to try if you had time, weren't afraid, didn't think you'd look silly, weren't too old or too young, too fat or too thin, etc.

1.

2.

3.

4.

5.

Now list the reasons you haven't tried them. Ask yourself, "How much of my life am I willing to give to that old idea?"

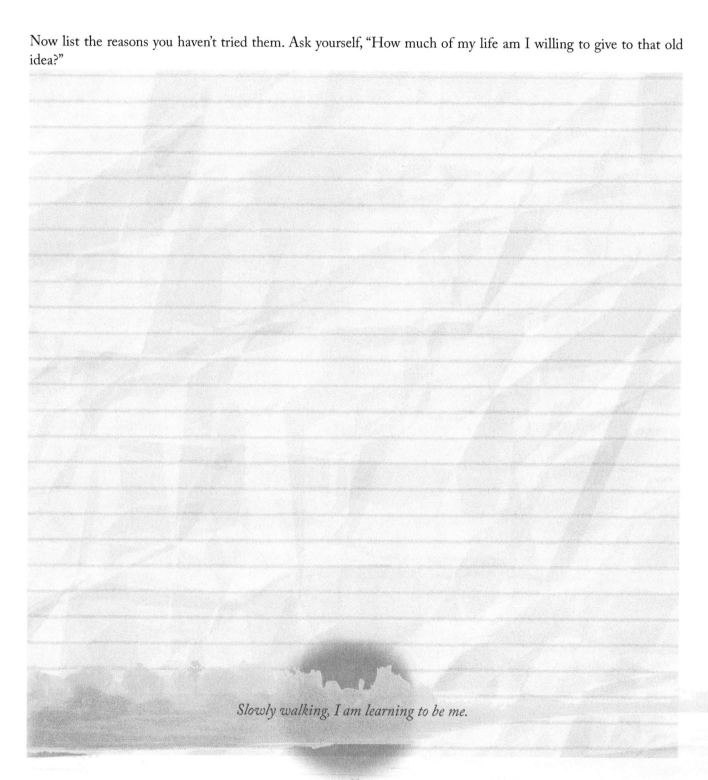

Slowly walking, I am learning to be me.

Notes

AND THEN THERE'S PARIS

Let yourself love with freedom and enthusiasm.

Have you ever visited a place that felt like home to you immediately? Why do you think it felt that way? Where did this feeling of homecoming originate? What have you learned from that?

What activities feel *like home* to you? Do you have a hobby or interest that you love enthusiastically? How does that affect your sense of self and/or of belonging? What does it teach you about yourself? Add a photo or drawing of something that feels like home to you.

I am not who I am because I am loved. I am who I am because I love.

Notes

THE PRINCESS AND THE PEA AND ME

I slowly began to nourish and accept my previously denied princess self.

What was your favorite fairy tale? Children's book? Bible story?
Why? What did you like about it as a child? Who or what in the story did you relate to most?

Have you ever had an insight about yourself that was sudden and unexpected? Did something trigger that insight? Write about the experience. If not sudden, how do you usually gain insight?

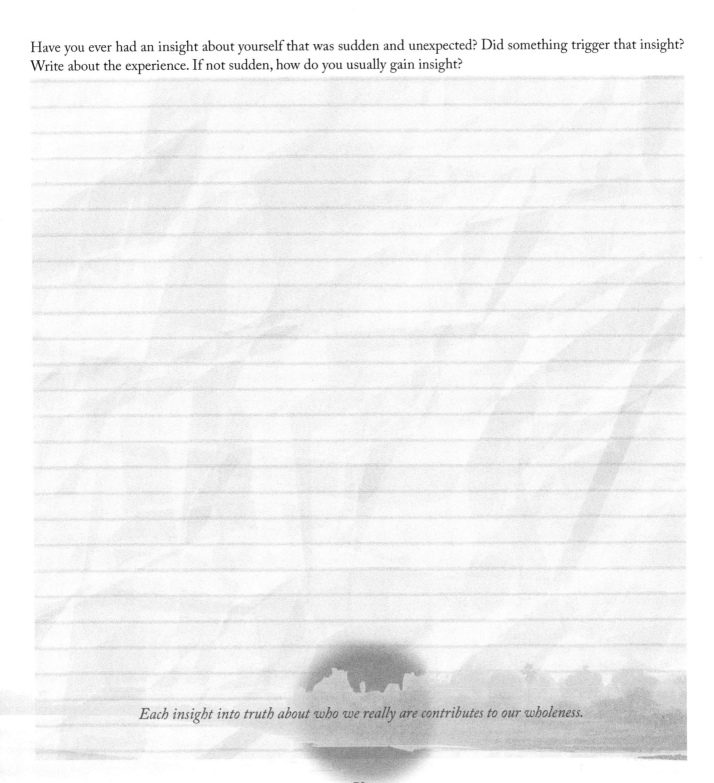

Each insight into truth about who we really are contributes to our wholeness.

Notes

A DREAM LIFE

Your dreams are your guides to the underworld of the psyche.

Do you recall a recurring dream you had at some time in your life or a theme that ran through several dreams? What was the dominant feeling tone of the dreams?

What is the one word your friends most often use to describe you? How accurate is that description? Just for fun, write the word's opposite and think about how it does or does not apply to you and your life.

Dreams never lie about feelings.

Notes

WHY NOT?

We must be brave enough to claim our beauty, our brilliance, our uniqueness,
and to find their proper expression in our lives.

Make a list of five beliefs that may have held you back from trying new things or pursuing a dream.

Make a list of the five things you fear most. Have those fears held you back in any way? Who or what might help you move past those fears if doing so seems realistic or helpful in some way.

Name one thing you would like to do if you thought you could.

At the heart of every problem is the unlived life.

Notes

BECOMING AWARE

Find someone who is honest and kind and tell your story.

Do you recall a time when you discovered an important insight about yourself that opened the door for change?

What factors or conditions contributed to the discovery of that insight?

Make no mistake: after insight, much work is required, but insight creates possibility.

Notes

TEACHING CATS TO SWIM

It's good to keep your eyes, ears, and mind open.

What are your five worst habits? What are your five best habits?

Make lists of your talents and weaknesses.

I am skilled/talented at: (Your list can be as long as it needs to be.)

1.

2.

3.

4.

5.

I am terrible at: (Your list can be as short as it needs to be.)

1.

2.

3.

4.

5.

Take your *terrible* list and think about each item. How do you know you are terrible at _____? Did someone tell you? Did you make a mistake? Did you fail?

Do you like doing _____ even though you think you're terrible at it? Would you be willing to try one of these again? What would you need to do differently this time?

Never be halfhearted about your loving.

Notes

Additional Thoughts . . .

We are each a living, breathing story in process with the authority to choose the next chapter. How marvelous is that!

WHERE DO I BELONG?

LEARNING TO LISTEN

The key is to learn what you love. Find the places, people, and activities that feel like home to you. There may be many or only a few. They will teach you about yourself and anchor you in the world. Let yourself love with freedom and enthusiasm. Never be halfhearted about your loving. Oh, yes, you might encounter disappointment. Someday, Paris may let me down. If that happens, I'll face it. But I refuse to deny myself the joy of wholehearted loving simply to protect myself from the pain of losing it.

How do you currently listen to the voice within? Give at least one example of a time of listening, what you learned, and how that changed you.

Is there a myth or traditional story that has helped you to gain greater insight about yourself or about the mysteries of life?

Set one small goal for living a more attentive life.

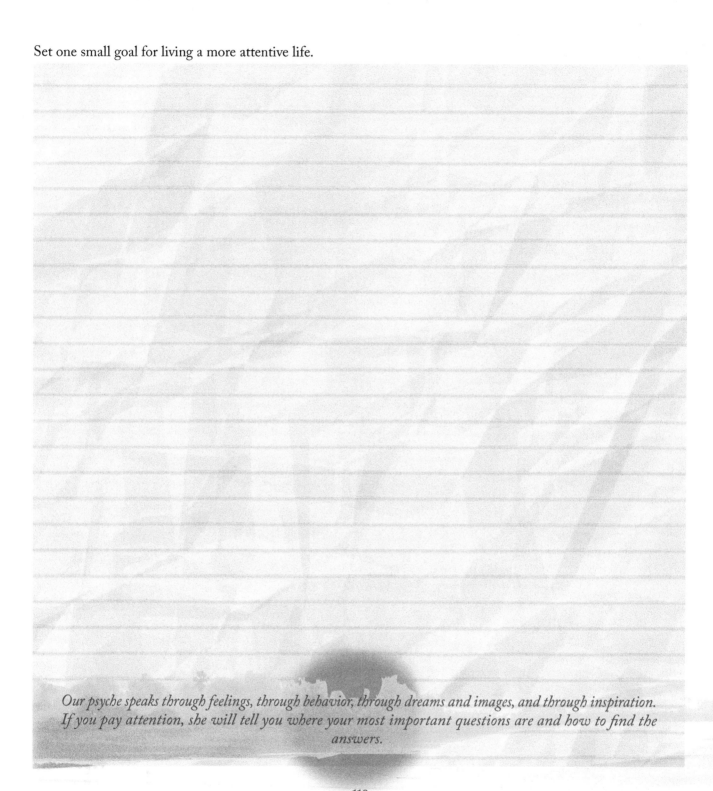

Our psyche speaks through feelings, through behavior, through dreams and images, and through inspiration. If you pay attention, she will tell you where your most important questions are and how to find the answers.

Notes

TIME AND PLACE

Become an anthropologist of your culture.

Where did you grow up? Describe that place as if to a stranger who has never been there. How did that place help shape who you are?

Describe your *fit* with your time and place of origin. What adjustments have you made, if any?

What is your favorite spot on earth? Why? What do you like to do there? How do you spend your time? What part of you—mind, body, heart, soul—does it connect to? Describe the life you would have if you lived there, if that's not your current residence or, if you do, how has being there changed you or helped you?

Where do you like to spend important holidays? With whom? Why?

Who are your favorite people? Make a list. Try to ignore your mind telling you who you should put on the list and just let it flow.

What is it about these people that make them favorites? How do you feel when you are with them?

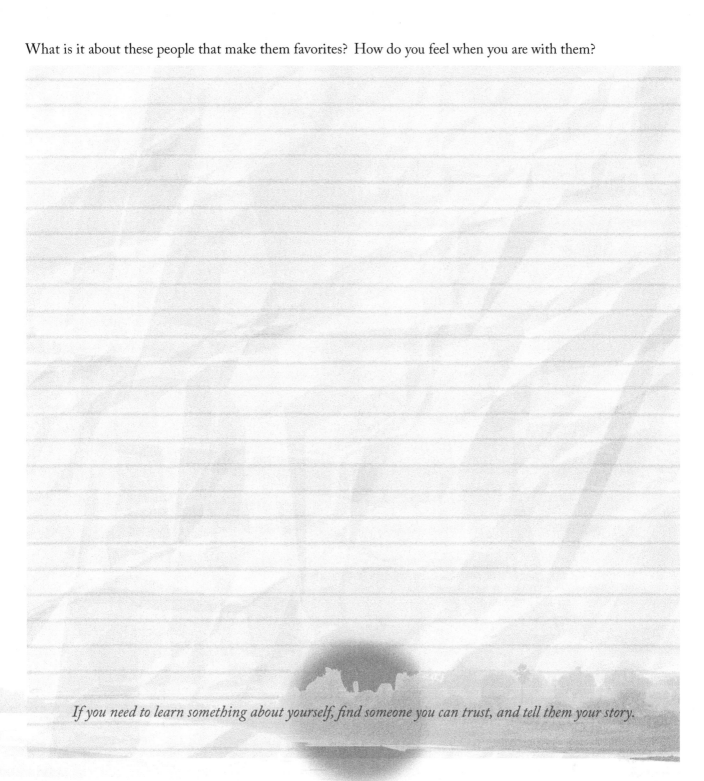

If you need to learn something about yourself, find someone you can trust, and tell them your story.

Notes

GOD'S GRACE

*What if God loves just loves you without reason, no matter
if you are good or successful or not?*

Give a few examples of *grace* in your life. How do you understand grace?

On what basis have you rested your sense of self-worth—the approval of others, accomplishments, performance, possessions, or qualities? Describe your experience.

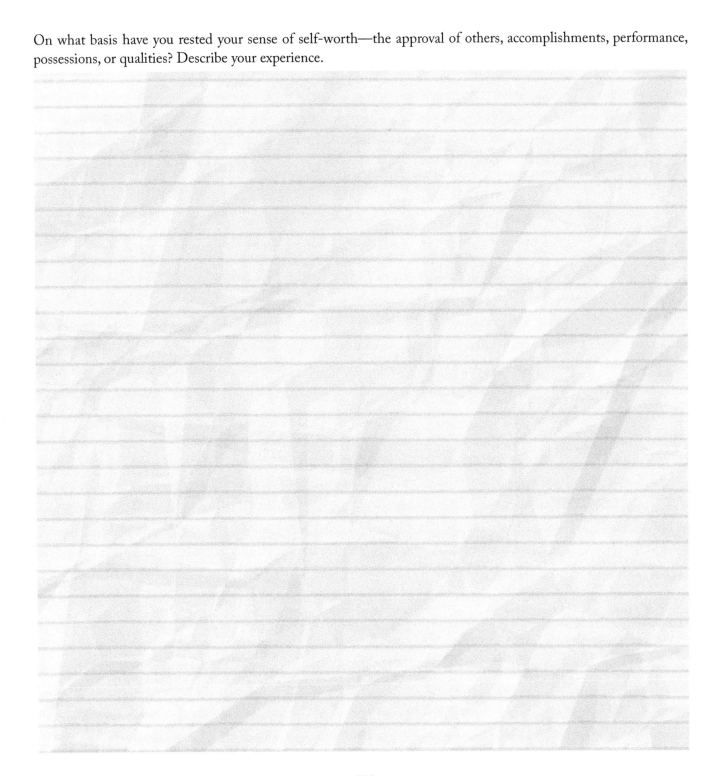

Can you imagine other ways of understanding self-worth?

Hope trumps certainty every time.

Notes

LOVE AND WORK

Work, defined broadly, is both the teacher and the lesson.

What activities make you smile, laugh out loud, cry with joy? What makes your heart sing? What were you doing the last time you lost track of time and totally got lost in the activity? How often do you engage with these interests? What stops you from doing them more frequently?

Addictions, fear, shame, arrogance, and pride often interfere with the flow of love. Are you aware of any barriers to love in your life right now? If so, write about these barriers and about what steps you might take to heal. If not, write about the experiences that led to being open to love.

What are your responsibilities at this point in your life? The list will include those things that are inherently yours—your health, happiness, spiritual life, how you treat others—and those you have either chosen or been assigned by someone else. Are there any that you should perhaps give up? Are there some that you have neglected? Are there some you need help with?

What is your dream job? Describe it in detail including the setting, how you would spend your time and with whom, what are its mission and objectives?

Go figure out what your love and work is and happiness will find you.

Notes

I HAD A DREAM

Listen to the dream and be curious about what it is trying to communicate.

Write the last dream you remember having in as much detail as you can but without interpreting it at all. What was the dominant feeling of that dream? What might that feeling have to teach you about yourself or your current life situation? Give the dream a title. You might also draw an image from it, make a collage, or write a poem, but find a creative way to express the images and feelings from your dream.

134

What is the earliest dream you recall? Write what you remember about how you felt when you awakened. Why do you think this dream has stayed with you? What would the adult-you say to the child who had that dream?

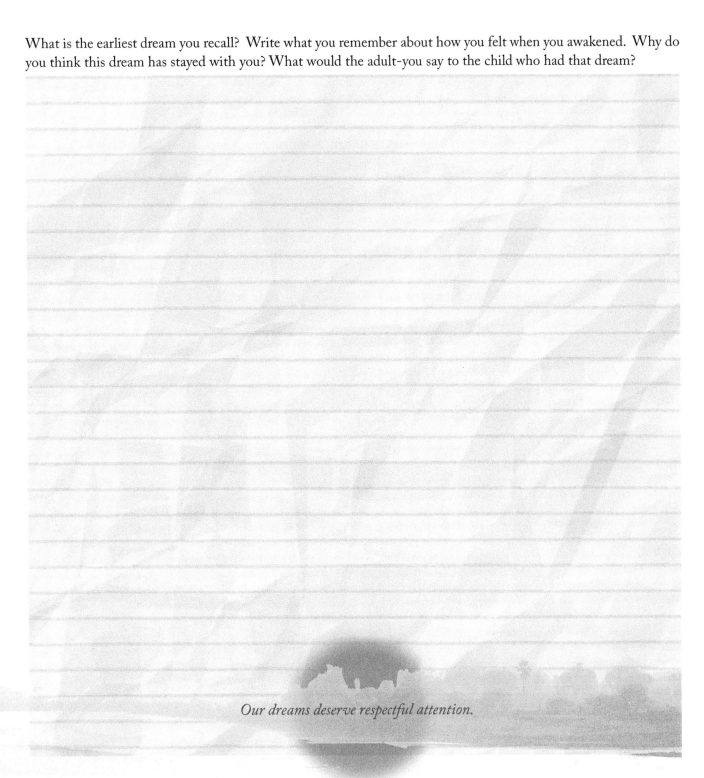

Our dreams deserve respectful attention.

Notes

THE OTHER KIND OF DREAM

The dream inside me had force, it had power, and it was good.

What do you dream of doing/being/seeing/feeling/accomplishing? Do you have a secret dream, one you've never told anyone or very few people about? Be specific. Give details. Write about it as if it's already happened or is happening now.

Have you ever attempted to fulfill a dream and failed? What happened? How did it feel? What did you learn?

Describe in detail a dream you have fulfilled. What happened? How did it feel? What did you learn? Add a photo or your own artwork that illustrates that accomplishment.

Be honest. Be bold. If your dreams seem totally unrealistic, they may be, but they are no less real and no less valuable for it. They hold the deepest knowledge of your purpose and promise and are guides to your wholeness. Dreams denied show up as symptoms or symbols. Pay attention to both. They will lead you to your truth.

Notes

WHAT'S IN A NAME?

Symbols have power. Your name is your first and most enduring symbolic representation.

How did you get your name? Who named you, and how did they choose? Are you named for someone? Who was that person? Do you like your name? If not, why not? If so, why?

Do you believe your name shaped you in any way? How or how not?

Is there a problem or situation in your life now that you are struggling to find a name for? Who or what can help with that?

When something new comes along, take care in its naming. It will matter.

Notes

HELPERS AND HEROES

Unexpected helpers appear just when we need them most.

Tell a story about one of your helpers.

Who are your heroes? What did that person do that seems heroic to you?

Write about a time when all seemed lost. What did you do? Who or what helped?

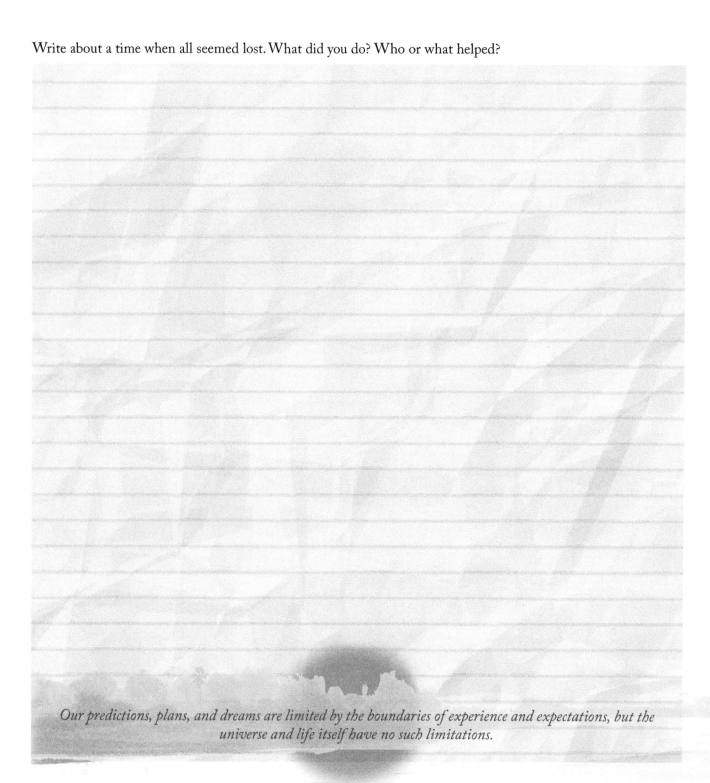

Our predictions, plans, and dreams are limited by the boundaries of experience and expectations, but the universe and life itself have no such limitations.

Notes

Additional Thoughts . . .

I discovered that the answers were within me. I would be defined and created by how I lived and how I loved.

PART IV

WHAT MATTERS?

MORE THOUGHTS ON STORY

We are given the power of observation and the possibility of choice. It is our responsibility to use this power to make our own best life.

Do you agree with the statement, *truth is in the story*? Why or why not?

What is a *true story* you can tell right now, on this page?

Who is a storyteller you love to listen to? What is one of your favorite stories this person tells? What do you gain from the story?

Facts are fine, but they don't have much to teach us until someone puts them into a story for us, or we do it for ourselves.

Notes

HOSPITAL BY THE SEA

For our souls to heal, we must care for our bodies and spirits.

In this Turkish story, the prescription for healing involved going to a healing place, making an offering of commitment, caring for the body and spirit, enlisting the aid of others, waiting for guidance, and telling the personal story of healing. Can you find elements of your own story in the Turkish one? Why or why not?

The hospital by the sea was a place of healing. Where has been a place of healing for you? How were you healed in this place? Include a photo or picture of your healing place here if you wish.

Have you had an important healing experience in your life? Write about that experience and what helped or hindered your healing. What lessons can you carry forward from that time?

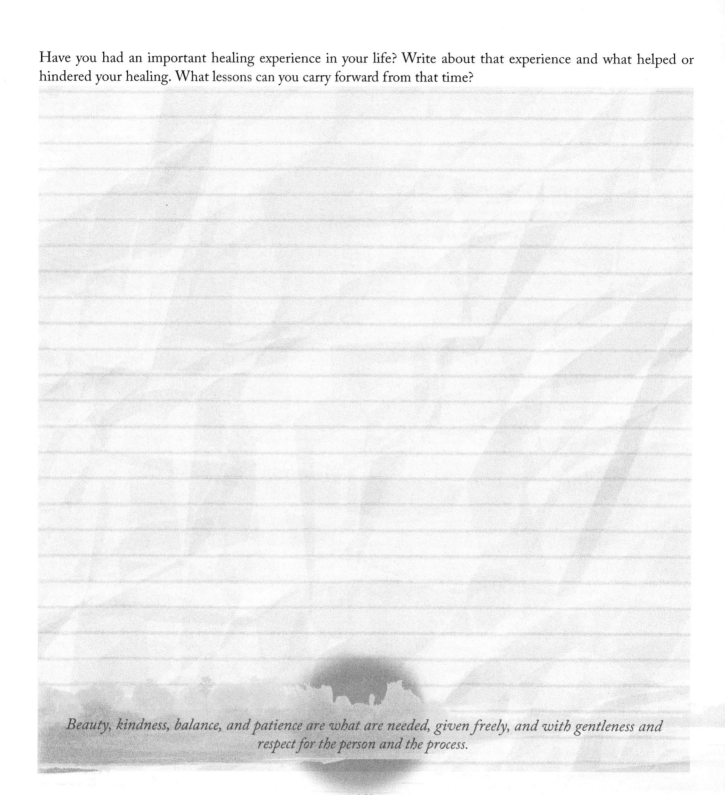

Beauty, kindness, balance, and patience are what are needed, given freely, and with gentleness and respect for the person and the process.

Notes

TELLING YOUR STORY

Each of us has a story inside our hearts, waiting to be told.

What story do you have waiting to be told? Where is a safe place to tell your story?

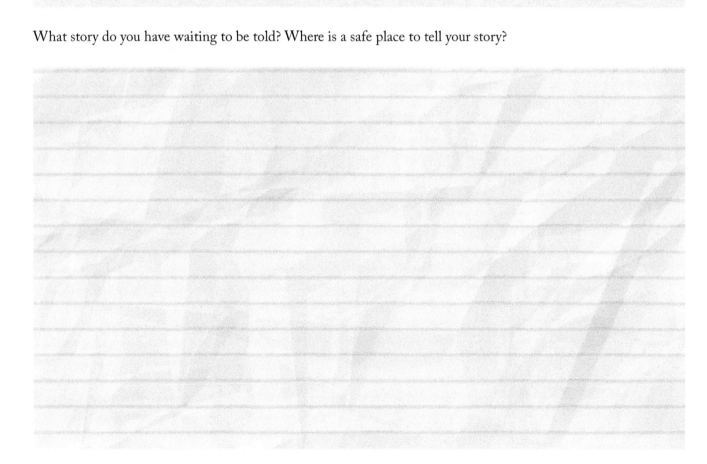

What would a *better you* look and feel like?

What is the first story you'd like to tell? Who will you tell it to? Write a draft of that story here.

The cure for what ails you begins with telling your story.

Notes

YOU CAN REFUSE TO BE A VICTIM

Our wounds...can certainly be made holy by our decision to use them for our spiritual growth.

Write about a time when you consciously chose not to be a victim to your circumstances. What happened? How did this impact your life and the way you felt about yourself?

What is something in your life today that isn't how you'd like it to be? What is one thing you can do to not be a victim to it?

What is one thing you can do to move past a difficulty in your life and use it as a means of spiritual growth?

Composer and musician Leonard Cohen says, "There is a crack in everything where the light can get in." What is the crack in your life where light can get in?

Was there a time in your life when you were injured or harmed and felt victimized? Write about that experience and how you have grown through it.

I can align myself with what is and proceed from that point with dignity, perseverance, and self-respect.

Notes

TOO BIG FOR YOUR BRITCHES

There is no shame in failure when we do our best but fail.

Do you remember a time when you were *too big for your britches?* What happened? What did you learn from this experience? How did it change you?

Do you agree that gratitude is a proper response to success? Why or why not?

Have you ever had a conscious feeling of gratitude as a response to success? Write about the circumstances surrounding this success and your response to it.

Write about a bit of *old wisdom* or *old truth* that was passed down to you from a parent, grandparent, teacher, or in some other way. How did you react at the time you were given the advice? How has it helped you in your life if it has or, if not, why not?

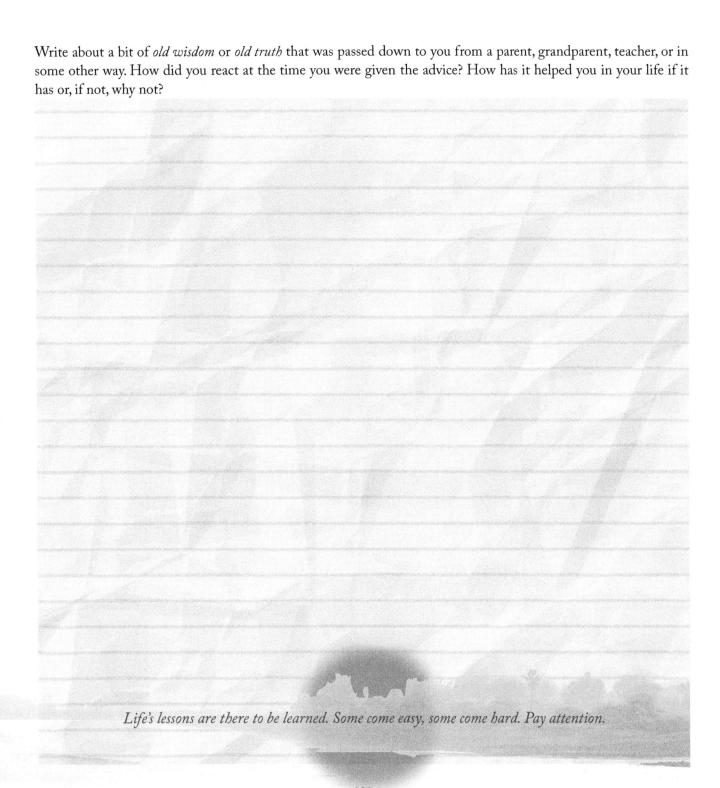

Life's lessons are there to be learned. Some come easy, some come hard. Pay attention.

Notes

OLD TRUTH

We need creativity to bring truth to us in a way that we can hear and use it.

Which of *The Four Agreements* resonates with you most? Why? Write about a situation that illustrates this agreement in action.

1. *Be impeccable with your word*

2. *Don't take anything personally*

3. *Don't make assumptions*

4. *Always do your best*

Which of *The Four Agreements* proves the most difficult for you? Why? Write about a situation that brought this difficulty to life for you.

When have you held an assumption that proved to be false? What happened? How did this impact you and your life?

As we travel along in life, all kinds of teachers pass our way. It's good to keep our eyes, ears, and minds open.

Notes

ON PRAYER

All our prayers are answered in precisely the ways that serve us best.

Do you believe in prayer? If so, how does prayer work in your life? If you do not believe in prayer, why not? Is there something else you do instead?

Do you believe prayers are answered in precisely the best way for you? Why or why not?

Have you had the experience of a prayer being answered in a way other than how you hoped? Describe the situation. Did the circumstances work out better in the end? Why or why not?

Do you work at expanding your faith? How do you do that?

What is your concept of God, a higher power, a guiding force, the universe, or whatever the entity is to whom you pray?

List five ways you currently nourish your spiritual life. Then list five ideas for enhancing your spiritual life. Choose one (or more) of these enhancements and make a plan for exploring it further.

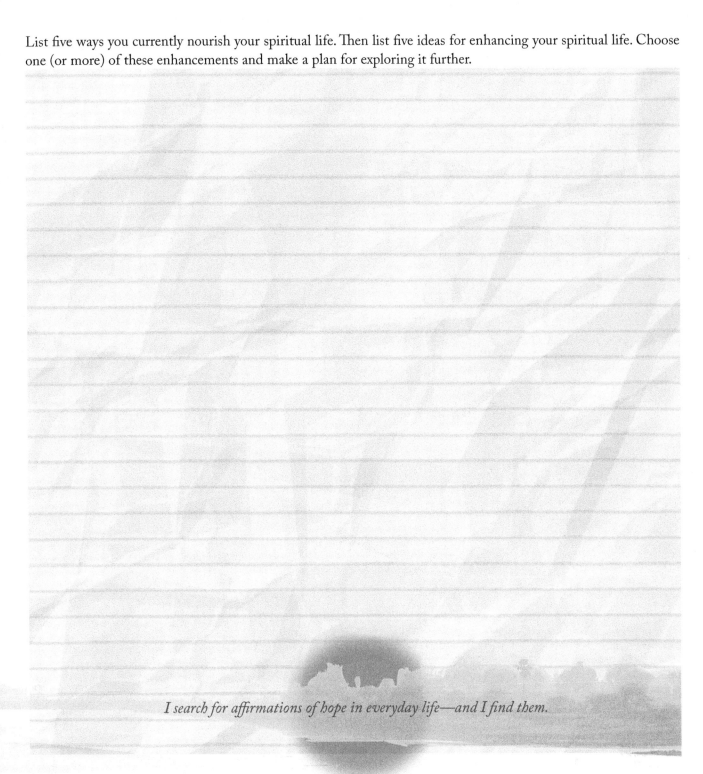

I search for affirmations of hope in everyday life—and I find them.

Notes

YOU GET TO CHOOSE

We get to choose the virtues we want to live by.

Make a list of the virtues you attempt to live every day. (If you'd like to review a list of virtues, see pages 148-150 in *Traveling Stories*.) What virtue on this list is most important to you? Which one is most difficult to live? Why?

What virtues do you want that you don't currently possess? What actions can you take to develop these virtues?

Where do you spend your time, energy, and money? Are these investments in line with the virtues you hold? Why or why not?

Who do you admire? Why? How are you like that person/not like that person?

Who do you want to be?

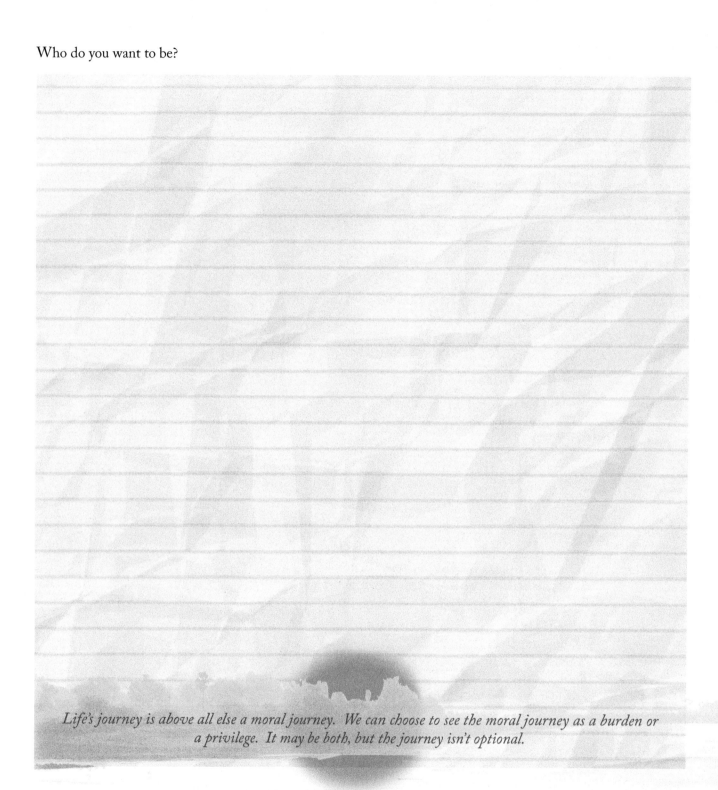

Life's journey is above all else a moral journey. We can choose to see the moral journey as a burden or a privilege. It may be both, but the journey isn't optional.

Notes

Additional Thoughts . . .

We need to couple compassionate insight and self-discipline to produce fundamental personality change.

PART V

HOW DO I LIVE MY LIFE?

HOW DO PEOPLE CHANGE?

Fall in love often, love well, do what's yours to do. Stay out of things that aren't yours.
Live with enthusiasm. Try hard. Always do your best. Be kind to others and yourself.
Let others take care of their own responsibilities. Do the next right thing.
Don't take yourself so seriously. Enjoy.

How do you think you've changed in the last ten years? Describe these changes in detail and then give a specific example of the old you versus the new you.

Have you ever experienced a sudden, dramatic change in who you are? What happened? What was the impact this change had on your life?

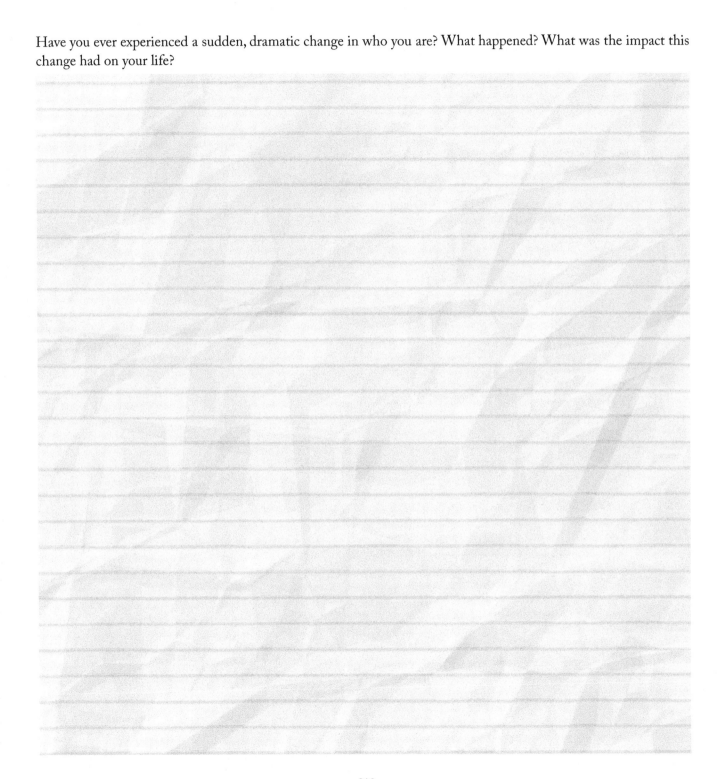

Do you believe all change is creative in nature? Why or why not?

What is it that you can do to prepare an *atmosphere of possibility* for the insight needed to change to come to you?

Can you recall an instance where you were given both a symptom and a symbol? What was the symptom that called your attention to the need for healing? What was the symbol that revealed the pathway to that healing? Add your own artwork or photo of the symbol that you've described.

Change will happen; our part is to stay connected to its process and be actively and lovingly involved in its emergence.

Notes

JUST HOW PERFECT DO YOU WANT TO BE?

How might you express your love, your vitality, your power, your energy, or your pain without the need to be perfect?

Do you struggle with perfectionism? If so, what does it look like in your life? How does it impact your relationships, work, joy, and other aspects of your life?

What are some actions you can take to let go of perfectionism, if it is something you struggle with?

If you don't struggle with perfectionism, what enables you to accept yourself and the world around you as it is? Provide an example of this acceptance in action.

What does *perfection* mean to you? How are you less than perfect in your own eyes? Make a list of five qualities you dislike in yourself. Then write about the positive side of that quality. What might you do to strengthen the positive aspect of those qualities and reduce the negative effects?

What might you say yes to?

Notes

FESTIVALS OF FORGIVENESS

I learned how human it is to be in need of forgiveness and a fresh start.

Who or what in your life needs forgiveness? You can spot these by how much time and negative energy you give to it each day. What is the cost of holding on? What might be the benefit of letting go?

What negative thought or action are you struggling with right now? What is one small action you can take to help let go of it?

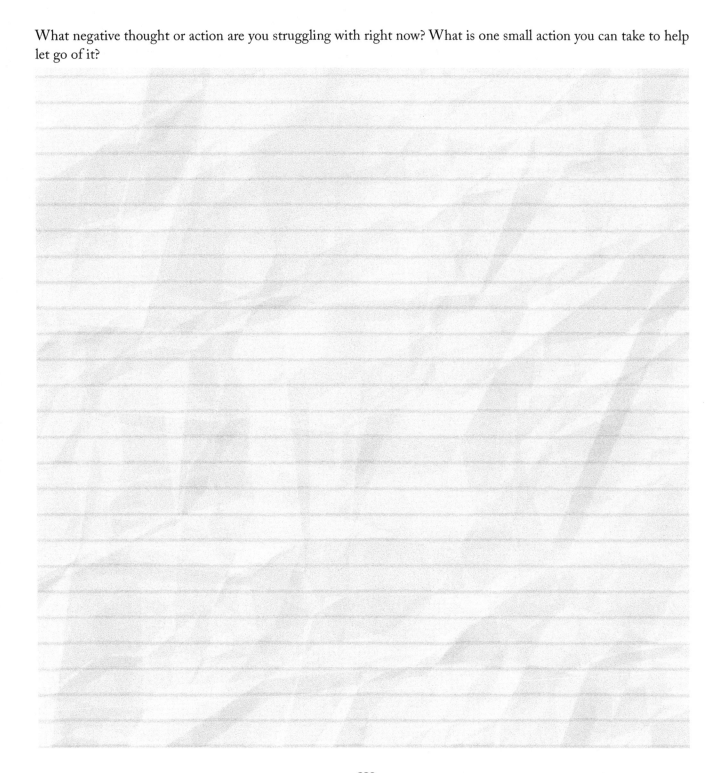

Rituals are how we mark transitions, affirm core beliefs and values, and enhance community. What rituals have been important for you in your life? Do you continue to practice these rituals or have they been lost to time, changing lifestyles, or personal choice?

Create a ritual, either a one-time ceremony to mark a transition, a birth, or a renewal, or an ongoing ritual to affirm core beliefs. Rituals can be simple or complex, but they should take place in a sacred space and time and will probably include words and objects that hold symbolic significance to you. Rituals may be solitary or include others. The only requirement is that they are meaningful to you and help you to connect more deeply with your truest intention.

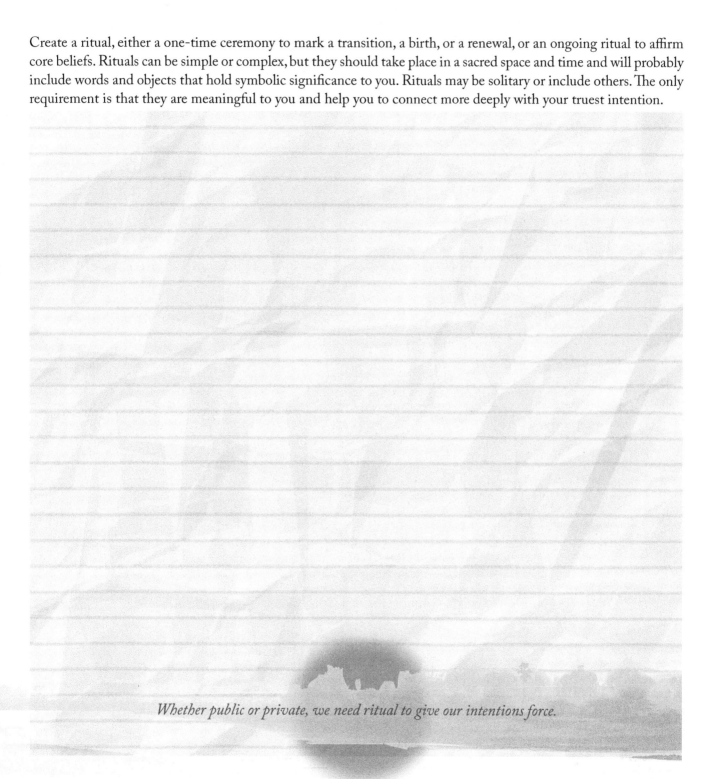

Whether public or private, we need ritual to give our intentions force.

Notes

JUST PLAY THE NOTES

What everyone can learn is that we don't need all the answers to our questions about life.

What does just play the notes look like in your life?

Do you value independence? How do you understand the limits of independence?

Do you feel that your own self reliance has at times failed you? Where have you turned for help in those instances?

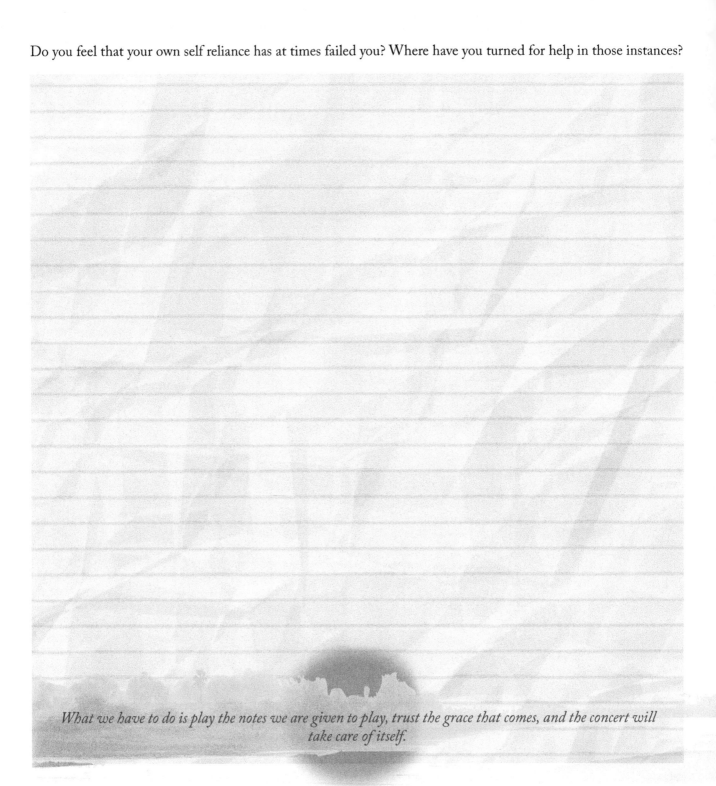

What we have to do is play the notes we are given to play, trust the grace that comes, and the concert will take care of itself.

Notes

HOLDING THE TENSION

Life is generous in its lessons.

What problem or conflict is facing you today? How might life be using this situation as an opportunity for growth? What might be the lesson you need to learn?

Is it difficult for you to hold the tension between two opposite forces and not rush to a decision? Why or why not? If you are currently in this position, write about the feelings involved in *not* making a choice.

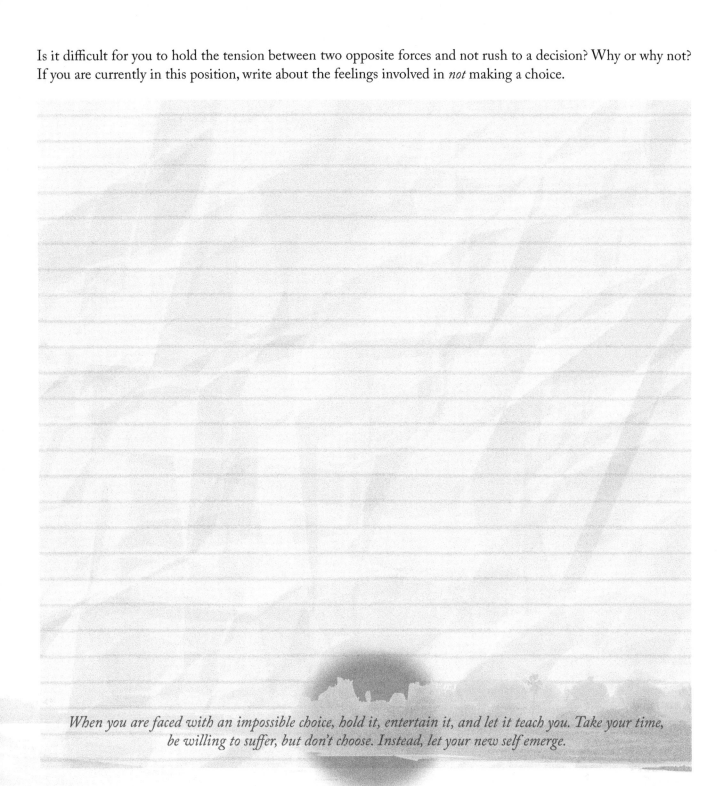

When you are faced with an impossible choice, hold it, entertain it, and let it teach you. Take your time, be willing to suffer, but don't choose. Instead, let your new self emerge.

Notes

STARFISH

Keeping is secondary; it's the finding and never knowing what will turn up that excites me.

What is your experience of the beach? What do you like or dislike about the beach? Describe a memorable moment you've had at the beach.

Can you remember looking for a sign and finding one? What was the sign? What did it symbolize for you? What did you do after receiving this sign? How did it impact your life?

What is the most unusual thing you've ever found or seen at the beach? Describe it in detail. How did you feel in this experience? What did it mean to you?

If you have a photo, add it here or create your own artwork.

Do you recall a time when a symbol appeared that opened your eyes to a previously unknown truth or possibility? Do you have one or more symbols or totems that you use to reinforce an important value of belief? Write about what symbols have meant for you so far and how you might use them more consciously in the future, if you see the value in that.

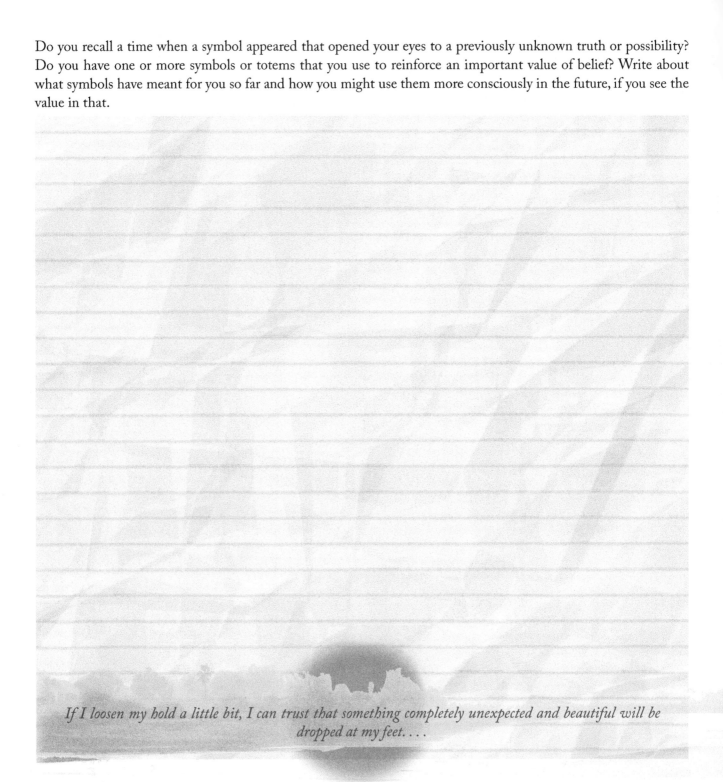

If I loosen my hold a little bit, I can trust that something completely unexpected and beautiful will be dropped at my feet. . . .

Notes

AND ANOTHER STARFISH

I trust that what comes next will be good, and I will know what to do when the time comes.

How do you usually deal with the so-called *negative emotions*—anger, jealousy, sadness, guilt and shame? Give an example from your life and consider what other options you may have.

What experiences have you had with synchronicity? Is synchronicity a regular part of your life or a once-in-a-while event? Describe one such instance in detail.

What can you do to make yourself more aware of symbols as they are presented in your life?

Does forgiveness come easily for you? Why or why not?

What were the circumstances surrounding a time you found it difficult to forgive someone? What happened? How did you resolve these feelings?

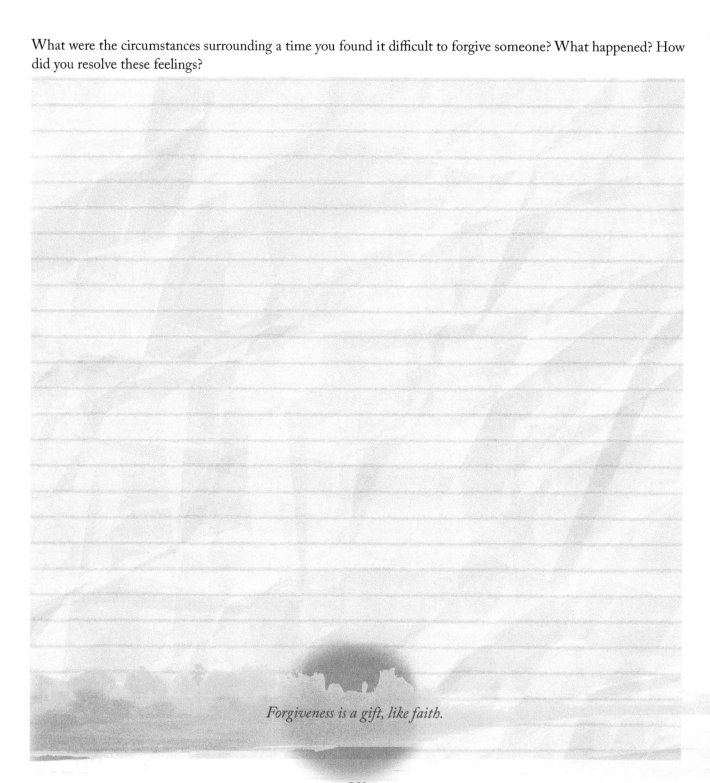

Forgiveness is a gift, like faith.

Notes

262

MOTHER TERESA & THE CRAZY OLD LADY

I had the answer to the question of what it would be like to be old.
The answer? Any way I wanted it to be.

When do you feel you are your most authentic self? Where are you? What are you doing? Who is you with?

Who was a teacher who appeared in your life at exactly the right moment? What did you learn from this person?

Are you waiting for a teacher now? What are you, as a student, doing to make yourself ready for this teacher to appear?

Have you ever had an encounter with someone famous? Who was the person and what were the circumstances surrounding this siting? Did you address the person? How did the interaction go?

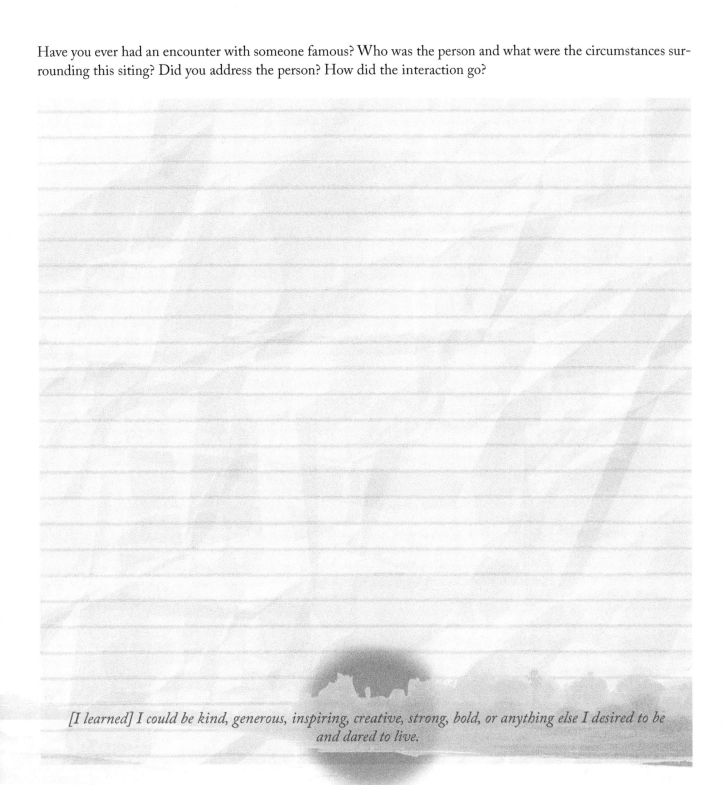

[I learned] I could be kind, generous, inspiring, creative, strong, bold, or anything else I desired to be and dared to live.

Notes

ANGEL ON THE GOLF COURSE

Somebody told me not to worry about the problems, but if you have to worry,
worry on the solution.

Do you believe in angels or other experiences that cannot be explained in ordinary practical terms? Why or why not?

Have you ever had a chance encounter when you were given the answer to a pressing question or were told something you badly needed to hear? If so, describe this encounter in detail. If not, would you like to have such an encounter? Why or why not?

Describe an experience that surprised you and perhaps opened your heart.

Knowing changes everything. Even one brief moment of faith can open a person's heart forever.

Notes

LITTLE YELLOW SPORTS CAR

When we learn to to own or acknowledge our own rage, we can use it to turn the injuries, hurts, or injustices upside down and make them right again.

What did you learn or what were you told about expressing anger?

Are you comfortable expressing anger? Why or why not?

How do you express your anger?

Is there something you'd like to do differently in how you express anger?

Is there a story within you waiting to be told? If so, when, where, and with whom will you share it?

No matter where you are in your life, when truth finds you, it is the right time to embrace it.

Notes

Additional Thoughts . . .

When we hear ourselves, and really listen to our stories, we will discover the myth we are living as well as the one we were meant to live. As a result, we are empowered to authorize how the tale goes forward.

EPILOGUE

TRAVEL WELL

TRAVEL WELL

We are always and forever in the process of creating our lives. The story we compose is made up of our circumstances, our choices, the lessons we are given, the lessons we seek, and what we make of it all. Life is going to happen. We choose how to participate with it. We can, if we want, become wholehearted participants, waiting with open hearts and minds for the lessons life offers and grabbing hold of what comes our way.

If you only had six possessions, what would they be? Why would you choose each item?

Do you look at envy as a positive or negative emotion? Explain. Has envy ever propelled you to accomplish something you would not have otherwise?

Envy is the feeling we have when we want something someone else has and we feel we lack—possessions, attributes, or qualities. What if the feeling of envy was sometimes a guidepost to our needed growth or hidden dreams? Is there someone you envy right now? If so, is this envy of possessions, qualities, or attributes? Is there something you can learn from this feeling?

Life is a journey. As we travel, old questions are answered and new ones emerge. This is the way of things, and it is good. List questions you can carry forward to the next part of your journey.

Use the rest of these pages to explore your stories as you wish and as you are inspired to do. Trust your instincts as well as the process.

Travel well. Be guided by your dreams and aspirations rather than your fears and expectations. Celebrate your lessons. Share your stories. Love and work, pray, pay attention, be honest, trust the process, and carry on. I wish you a wonderful trip.

Notes

Additional Thoughts . . .

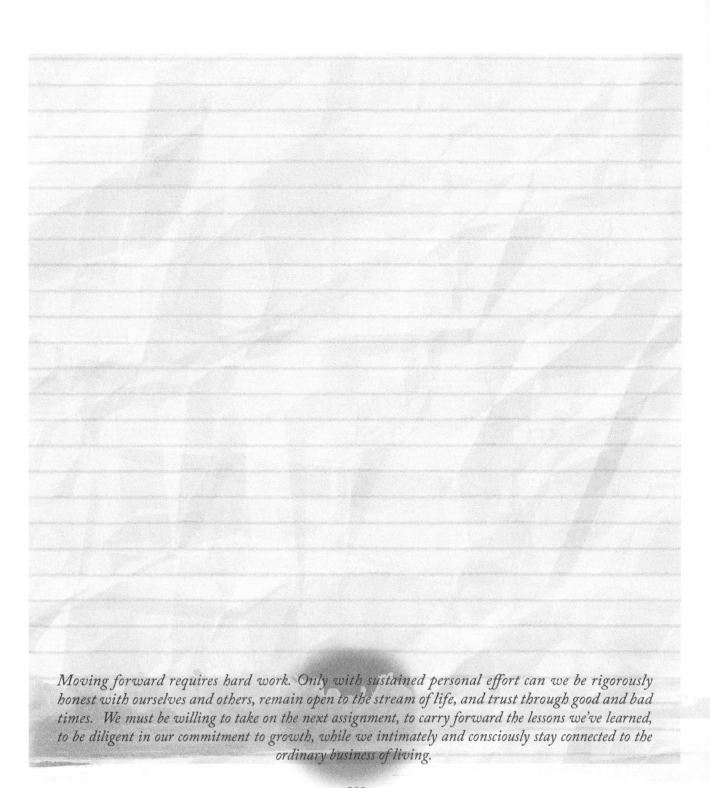

Moving forward requires hard work. Only with sustained personal effort can we be rigorously honest with ourselves and others, remain open to the stream of life, and trust through good and bad times. We must be willing to take on the next assignment, to carry forward the lessons we've learned, to be diligent in our commitment to growth, while we intimately and consciously stay connected to the ordinary business of living.

ABOUT THE AUTHOR

TERRI CLEMENTS DEAN, PhD, is a clinical psychologist in private practice and a popular lecturer. A former anthropologist, she has studied deeply in philosophy, belief systems, gender knowledge, and psychology with a particular focus on symbolic systems. She was Clinical Director for Safe Recovery Systems and regional director for Georgia Highlands Mental Health Systems before working exclusively with private psychotherapy clients. Her broad interests and extensive mental health experience give her a unique perspective in understanding each person's life as well as a deep well of resources to guide her work as a clinician, lecturer, and writer.

She believes that wholeness is our birthright and that life is a journey toward claiming our deepest, best selves. Find more about what she's learned on her journey at www.TerriDean.us.

Her book, *Traveling Stories: Lessons from the Journey of Life* is available in paperback through her website, from Amazon.com, and as an e-book from most e-book outlets, including Kindle, Nook, and iBooks.

Terri lives in North Florida with her husband, Mark.

Contact Terri at terri@terridean.us. She welcomes your stories.